Navigating at Sea

Dona Herweck Rice

Smithsonian

Contributing Author

Allison Duarte, M.A.

Consultants

Tamieka Grizzle, Ed.D.
K–5 STEM Lab Instructor
Harmony Leland Elementary School

Russ Lee
Curator
Smithsonian

Publishing Credits

Rachelle Cracchiolo, M.S.Ed., *Publisher*
Conni Medina, M.A.Ed., *Managing Editor*
Diana Kenney, M.A.Ed., NBCT, *Content Director*
Véronique Bos, *Creative Director*
June Kikuchi, *Content Director*
Robin Erickson, *Art Director*
Seth Rogers, *Editor*
Mindy Duits, *Senior Graphic Designer*
Smithsonian Science Education Center

Image Credits: pp.2–3, p.10 (all), p.16 (right), p.18 (all), p.20 (bottom left), p.21 (top) © Smithsonian; p.5, p.13, p.22 Timothy J. Bradley; p.6 Granger Academic; p.7 Public domain; p.8 Inge Wallumrød/Pexels; p.11, p.12 Look and Learn/Bridgeman Images; p.14 Science Source; p.15 Mark Garlick/Science Source; p.17 Colaimages/Alamy; p.19 Andrew Brookes, National Physical Laboratory/Science Source; p.23 Universal History Archive/UIG/Bridgeman Images; p.26 (bottom) Richard Howard/The LIFE Images Collection/Getty Images; p.27 (top) Edmond Terakopian/AFP/Getty Images; all other images from iStock and/or Shutterstock.

Library of Congress Cataloging-in-Publication Data

Names: Rice, Dona, author.
Title: Navigating at sea / Dona Herweck Rice.
Description: Huntington Beach, CA : Teacher Created Materials, [2018] | Audience: K to grade 3. | Includes index.
Identifiers: LCCN 2017060488 (print) | LCCN 2017061409 (ebook) | ISBN 9781493869206 (e-book) | ISBN 9781493866809 (pbk.)
Subjects: LCSH: Navigation--History--Juvenile literature. | Navigation--Technological innovations--Juvenile literature. | Seafaring life--Juvenile literature. | Ocean travel--Juvenile literature.
Classification: LCC VK559.3 (ebook) | LCC VK559.3 .R53 2018 (print) | DDC 623.89--dc23
LC record available at https://lccn.loc.gov/2017060488

Smithsonian

Teacher Created Materials

5301 Oceanus Drive
Huntington Beach, CA 92649-1030
www.tcmpub.com

ISBN 978-1-4938-6680-9
© 2019 Teacher Created Materials, Inc.
Printed in China 51497

Table of Contents

Second Star to the Right

Peter Pan follows the stars to Neverland. "Second star to the right and straight on till morning!" he cries as he **navigates** the sky. He leads his group toward a grand adventure. The stars tell him just where to find it.

Neverland is not real, of course. But following the stars is. It was one of the first ways people learned to navigate. They followed the stars both on sea and on land. They used stars to position themselves. Then, they could figure out where they needed to go.

Instruments have changed over time. Better and better technology is used. It is more precise than it has ever been. But the roots of navigation remain. In many ways, we still follow the stars.

early navigation instruments

find his position at sea.

By Land, By Sea

Since they first walked, people have been on the move. They travel to explore new areas. This has always been easiest by land. People can walk across land and rest when they need to. They can find food and water along the way. They can use landmarks as guideposts.

Traveling by sea is riskier than traveling by land. The sea is always changing. There are few landmarks that stay in one place on the water. It is not as easy to find resources out in the sea. The sea itself is full of dangers. People cannot just swim through the water and rest when needed.

This 1773 engraving shows villagers from Tahiti traveling by boat.

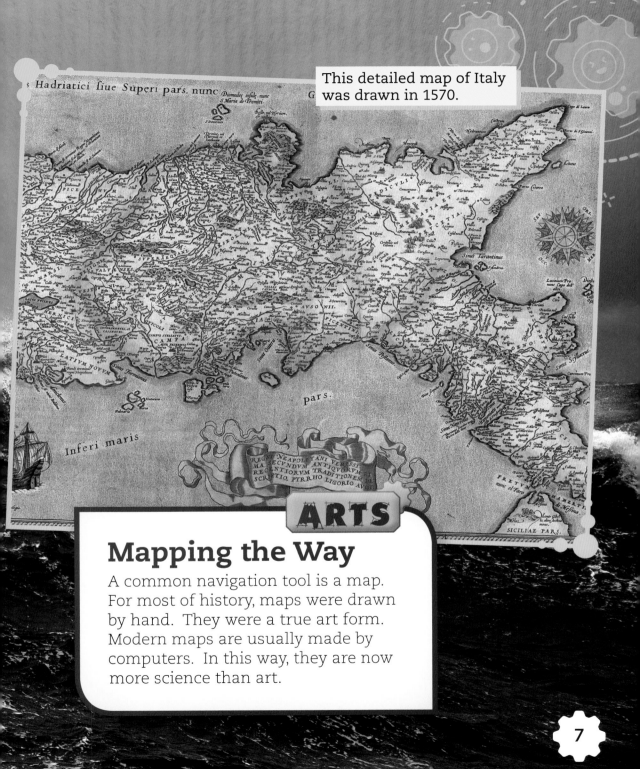

This detailed map of Italy was drawn in 1570.

Mapping the Way

A common navigation tool is a map. For most of history, maps were drawn by hand. They were a true art form. Modern maps are usually made by computers. In this way, they are now more science than art.

Latitude and Longitude

To pinpoint their location, people made an invisible grid around Earth. This grid is made of two sets of lines. Lines of latitude circle Earth from east to west. These lines are **parallel**. They never cross each other. The center line is the equator.

Lines of longitude run north and south. These lines are not parallel. They meet at the poles. These lines are also called *meridians*. The center line is the prime meridian. Both sets of lines are measured in **degrees**. With degree **coordinates**, any spot on Earth can be found.

Early navigators could use this grid to help them—if they could figure it out at sea. They began to make tools to help them find what they needed to know.

Navigation is from the Latin word *navis*, which means "ship." To navigate is to steer a ship.

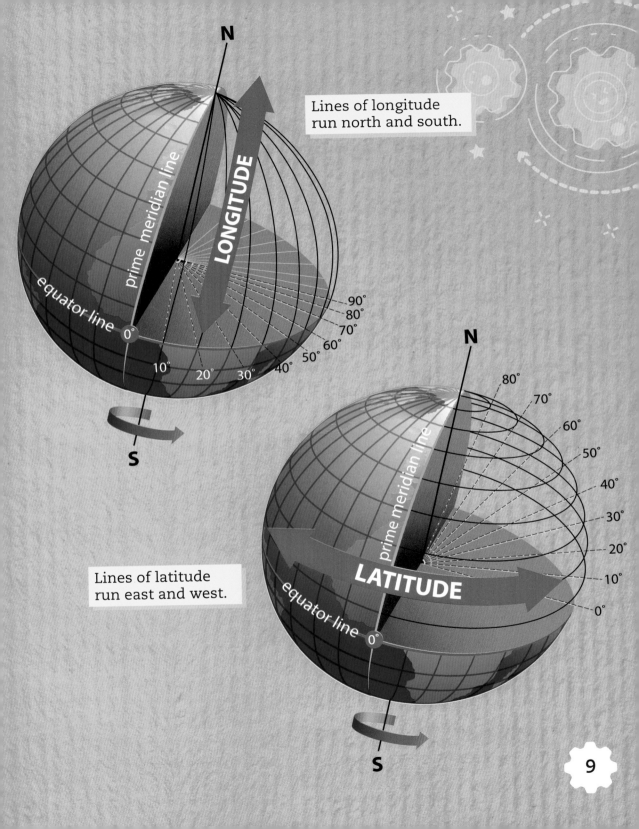

N

Lines of longitude
run north and south.

prime meridian line

LONGITUDE

equator line

0°

10°   20°   30°   40°   50°   60°   70°   80°   90°

S

N

prime meridian line

LATITUDE

equator line

0°

80°   70°   60°   50°   40°   30°   20°   10°   0°

Lines of latitude
run east and west.

S

Early Navigation

It is human nature to want to explore. People want to know what is beyond what they see. By 1700, people from Europe had explored about half of Earth's surface. But there was so much more to know!

It was hard enough to explore the land. The seas posed even more challenges. Even so, the risks seemed worth it. People were sure that opportunities waited for them. Wealth and power could be gained in and across the waters. One problem was how to plot a sea route. **Open water** was filled with danger. People had to get where they were going quickly. Sailing without a clear route was too risky. People needed tools they could trust.

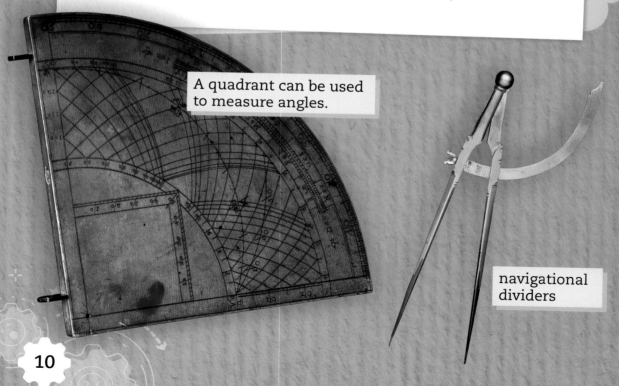

A quadrant can be used to measure angles.

navigational dividers

This sailor uses tools to navigate.

In open water, sailors used **dead reckoning** to figure out their location in the water. It is based on the last location, direction, and speed traveled.

Viking Sunstones

Vikings sailed the seas long ago. They visited many lands and traded for what they needed. They **raided** some places, too. Vikings were known for their fierceness and skills at sea.

Vikings developed tools and methods to help them navigate. They were experts at using the sun to find direction. This was hard to do where they lived. The skies were often overcast and foggy. They found a solution with sunstones. Sunstones are crystals that polarize, or control, light. They helped Vikings find the sun when there were clouds in the sky. At least they had some idea of their direction.

But "some idea" was not good enough. They needed a more precise way to know where they were headed. They soon found it.

a Viking at sea

SCIENCE

The direction of light polarization in the sunstone matches the polarization of the sunlight.

The atmosphere polarizes light in a circular pattern.

The sun is hidden behind clouds.

1 The navigator points a sunstone at a patch of sky and twists it until it appears brightest. The crystal now points toward the sun.

2 The navigator repeats the process from another position. The intersection of the two readings show the sun's location.

Lodestones

Compasses have been around a long time. They are used to find direction. But before them, there were lodestones.

Lodestones are pieces of magnetic ore. They are found in nature. Vikings used lodestones to make magnets. They rubbed needles on lodestones. This magnetized the needles. In other words, the needles became magnets.

Magnets have a force that attracts and repels. Magnet ends attract or repel other magnets. Earth has a magnetic field. A magnet can align to, or line up with, Earth's magnetic field.

Vikings placed a charged needle in a bowl of water. It floated. It slowly pointed north and south. It aligned with Earth's magnetic field. They could then "read" the needle.

magnetic stone

Earth and its magnetic field

Magnetic force is strongest at a magnet's north and south poles. This is true of Earth, too!

Sextants

In the late 1600s, King Charles of England gave scientists a task. He asked them to use objects in the sky to find where they were. They made a tool called a sextant.

A sextant measures the angle between two objects. The user looks at the horizon through an eyepiece and a half mirror. One more mirror is placed on a moving arm. It is moved until the reflection of the sun (or star) seems to meet the horizon. Then, the angle between the two objects is measured. A sextant's scale is used for this. The angle can be used to find the user's location and distance.

In time, better sextants were made. They became more precise. Scientists could find a location within one degree of latitude. They could find distance almost exactly.

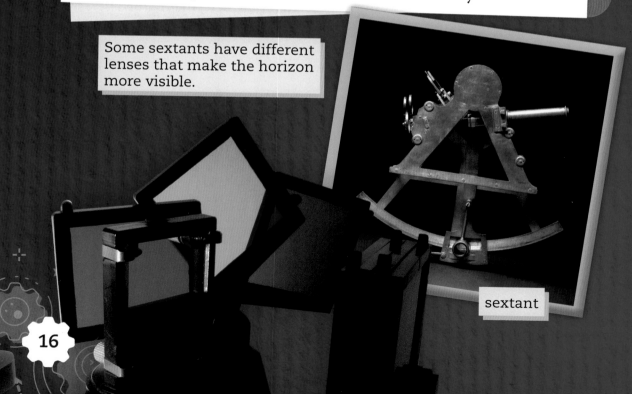

Some sextants have different lenses that make the horizon more visible.

sextant

This sailor uses a sextant.

MATHEMATICS

Measuring Degrees

One degree of latitude is 111 kilometers (69 miles). To use a sextant, angles are compared to tables with degrees of latitude. Without the tables, location would remain a mystery.

Longitude and a Good Clock

By about 1700, people could easily find latitude at sea. They had tools to rely on. But longitude was not the same. They needed seaworthy clocks. This is why: Earth **rotates** 15 degrees of longitude each hour. People at sea could only find longitude by comparing ship time to the time on clocks they brought from land. Ship time was found with the sun. But land clocks did not keep time well on ships. These clocks had **pendulums**. The ships and clocks bobbed about on the sea. This affected the clocks.

But it was just a matter of time before a good sea clock was invented! Countries began to offer big prizes for a great clock. Many people tried. Soon, the **marine chronometer** (kruh-NAW-muh-tuhr) was made. It kept accurate time at sea. Now, both longitude and latitude could be found.

Clocks like this do not keep time well at sea.

marine chronometer

Clocks continue to improve. The device above is a clock that is so accurate that it would take 20 million years for it to be just one second slow!

Navigation Now

As the 1800s came to an end, navigation tools were better than they had ever been. Maps were reliable. Tools could be relied on. Math knowledge had advanced, too. People could make more precise calculations. This meant they could find more precise locations. They could sail the seas with confidence. They knew where they were and where they were going.

But something big was about to happen. Air travel and space travel began. An even greater need for precise navigation came with them. New tools were made to meet the demand. They helped people fly through the air. They helped with sea travel, too.

space shuttle

early airplane

This gimbal makes sure the disc in the center does not move when the ship does.

TECHNOLOGY

Gimbal

Scientists needed to find a way to keep instruments steady on moving ships. They turned to gimbals. A gimbal is a set of rings in which an object can be mounted. Each ring pivots on its own. The object is mounted to the center ring by a center **axis**. Each outer ring is mounted to another by two axis points. The gimbals pivot, but the object stays steady.

21

Radio

One of the biggest changes in navigation was communication. Radio was a **vital** new tool. Information could be sent to ships from land or between ships. Ships could ask for help, too. In the past, a big threat to ships was being alone at sea. There was no way to get help if something happened. Being able to reach out beyond the ships made it safer for all.

The U.S. Navy began to send time signals to its ships by radio. This time communication was more exact than before. Warnings were also shared with ships. Perhaps a storm was on its way. Maybe danger was near. With radio, news could be shared no matter where a ship was. Ships were not alone. And navigating was not as hard.

radio tower on a ship

Guglielmo Marconi (left), inventer of the radio, uses one of his early machines.

Radio waves can travel through walls, people, and other objects!

GPS

When people think of navigating today, they think of GPS. It stands for Global Positioning System. It has changed how people find their way.

GPS uses 24 satellites that orbit Earth. Each one orbits Earth twice a day. There are at least four satellites in range at all times over any point on Earth. Each one sends and receives signals. A GPS receiver reads those signals. The device can read a location almost anywhere in the world.

Many people have a GPS device in their smartphones. They have GPS in their cars. It is often used for directions. Ships now have GPS. They can always find their way. They can always be found, too!

GPS satellites circle Earth on different paths.

Sails use wind to push a boat forward.

ENGINEERING

Go, Boat, Go!

Like GPS, different instruments have been made to tell sailors where they are and where to go. But sailors still need to be able to make their boats move. Engineers design boats using basic tools. Some boats have sails, so wind can push them. Some have motors or engines. Some even have paddle wheels.

Straight on till Morning

Where there is a will, there is a way. People want to explore the waters of the world, as they have for thousands of years. In that time, people have found better and more precise ways to travel the seas. They have gone from sailing along the shore to crossing open water. They have tracked their paths by the stars and the sun. Today, they use GPS. People will continue to explore into the future.

What will the future hold? Things have changed so much over time. It makes sense that they will continue to change. New tools will be invented. New methods will be used. And as Peter Pan declares, people who travel the seas can sail "straight on till morning." Maybe then they will find what they are looking for!

In 1990, William "Bill" Pinkney became the first African American, and the fourth person in the world, to sail around the globe alone.

In 2006, Dee Caffari became the first woman to sail solo, nonstop around the world.

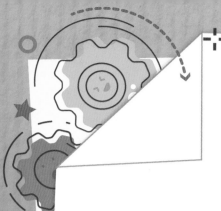

STEAM CHALLENGE

Define the Problem

You are on a ship traveling across the ocean when suddenly the navigational equipment for the ship breaks down! You know that you need to travel north to get to the closest shore. Your task is to build a device that will help you find north. Then, you can figure out the best plan to navigate the ship safely to land.

Constraints: The items you have to work with are: a pencil, paper, a magnet, paperclips, a plastic cup, a bowl, water, string, bamboo skewers, and a cork.

Criteria: A successful device will be able to rotate and clearly point north.

Research and Brainstorm

How have people found north in the past? Which methods will work best on a ship at sea?

Design and Build

Create a plan for how you will use the materials to find north. What purpose will each part serve? What materials will work best? How will you make it clear which direction is north? Build the model.

Test and Improve

Test your device by using it to point north. Then, use a compass or a map to tell if the device is successful. Did you find north? How might you improve your plan? Modify your design, and try again. If your design was successful, try a different method.

Reflect and Share

How might your plan change if you needed to travel at night? How would your plan change if you needed to travel east instead of north? Which part of the process was most challenging?

Glossary

axis—straight line around which something turns

coordinates—a set of numbers used to locate a point on a line, on a surface, or in space

dead reckoning—figuring out a ship's position based on its speed and the distance traveled

degrees—units of measurement in lines of latitude and longitude

magnetic ore—earth materials that contain metals that push away and attract magnetic materials

marine chronometer—clock designed for use at sea

navigates—figures out how to go from one place to another

open water—areas in the ocean far from shore where no land can be seen

parallel—extending in the same direction and the same distance apart, but never touching at any point

pendulums—sticks or strings with weights at the bottoms that swing back and forth

raided—broke into and stole from

repels—pushes away

rotates—turns on a center

vital—necessary

Index

Do you want to help people cross oceans?
Here are some tips to get you started.

"Learn as much as you can about math and science. And, if you like to think creatively and solve problems, study engineering and technology." **—Dan Cole, Geographic Information Systems Coordinator**

"GPS transmitters and receivers are shrinking in size and power requirements. So understanding microelectronics is essential. More and more people will navigate using artificial intelligence." **—Russ Lee, Chair, Aeronautics Division, National Air and Space Museum**